THE WHEEL OF THE YEAR SERIES

PREMONITION
— DESIGNS —

Fleurdelys
COVENSTEAD

EST. 2017

pine
& parchment

CHILDREN'S INTRO TO
IMBOLC

AN ILLUSTRATED GUIDE

BY LIAM CAREW

Welcome to the village by the pond!
This time of year - it's the place to go!
What once was a quiet fishing spot,
is now a playground of ice and snow!

My neighbors and I are celebrating Imbolc,
a holiday of potential and possibilities!
We're so glad that you'll be joining us,
there's so many wintery wonders to see!

I'm sure you've heard of
Groundhog's Day,
but were you also aware,
that Imbolc inspired that holiday,
based on an animal we hold so dear!

Because this is a holiday of possibility,
predicting the weather is on theme;
We turn to the Groundhog,
for their gift of prophecy,
to signal Winter's potential shift to Spring.

The Groundhog also symbolizes truth,
and that honesty is the way to go!
Don't hold back on sharing how you feel,
and tell your loved ones
what they need to know!

Through the truth, you'll form a bond,
like a Wolf does with its pack.
On Imbolc we celebrate these beasts,
because they always have eachother's backs

Wolves are symbolic of friendship and family,
and of other relationships built in trust.
A reminder that with respect for one another,
the possibilities are endless for us!

The pack survives and thrives,
by focusing on each individual's skills;
A metaphor that every single person
has something to contribute,
when encouraged to their full potential.

What skills do you have
that your friends and family appreciate?

Serpents get such a bad wrap,
often accused of being dishonest...
But these reptiles also represent truth,
just the dark truths that no one
wants to discuss.

As people we are not perfect,
there are cravings and urges hard to control.
Like, wanting to play with your toys at bed time,
or eating sweets even when you're told no.

A Serpent represents shedding those behaviors,
just as they shed their skin;
Understanding that this part of you exists,
but as you mature,
you will not let every impulse win!

What behavior, if any, are you trying to shed?

Swans, like serpents,
remind us to turn inward;
To love ourselves for all that we are.
We are growing through imperfection,
but we deserve self-love, for sure!

Swans are the ultimate symbol of winter,
they are beautiful and full of charm.
But just like this frigid, frozen season,
do not assume by their peaceful appearance,
that they will not cause harm.

Swans are devoted protectors,
their family takes priority,
but only after they've ensured,
that they've taken care of themselves properly.

A good reminder to work on yourself -
Your needs are as important as any one elses!

You may see less birds
or new kinds you're not used to,
but that's no reason to be alarmed!
Birds migrate from one place to another -
This keeps them strong and warm!

Two ways to welcome our feathered friends,
is to give them shelter and feed them well!
I have a variety of bird houses out back,
and I leave snacks right where they dwell.

But a fun way to give them seeds,
is to take pinecones inside,
add a ribbon and cover with peanut butter,
then dip them in seeds on all sides!

Hang the pinecones from a tree,
and watch the birds chirp in glee as they feed!

It is so much fun to play in the snow!
There is really so much to do!
You can sled, make snow angels,
make snow people, or even build an igloo!

Another thing is how awesome it all looks,
to see a familiar place look brand new!
The white snow adds a blanket to everything,
nature creating a beautiful, icy view!

If you don't get snow where you live,
I understand you may not relate,
but you can always use crafting supplies,
to make paper snowflakes!
And depending how you look at it,
consider yourself lucky - it isn't always fun;
In fact, when it snows,
there's always chores, like shoveling, to be done!

Whether frozen or not,
without water, there wouldn't be life...
And so, on Imbolc, to honor this liquid gift,
we decorate a water feature outside!

For us, that means we decorate a well,
despite it being old and no longer functional.
It is still a symbol of water and life,
and so, it receives a festive overhaul!

Not all neighbors have wells,
so they decorate bird baths or spheres of ice.
They do so with flowers, figurines, or ribbons,
or freezing layers of water with different
colored dyes!

What would you do if you did this at home?
Do you have something to decorate
or would you need to make your own?

Heading back indoors,
we find warmth in many ways.
One of which is candle making,
an old art we partake in on this holiday!

For some folks, today is called Candlemas.
As you can guess, candles take center stage.
We also celebrate these waxy items,
but do so with an energy exchange:

Think of a loved one, and make them a wish!
Melt down the wax, add in a scent!
Pour it into a mold with a wick,
and manifest your intent!

Give it away,
and tell them what you desired;
Knowing that when they light it,
your wish, for them, is enhanced by the fire!

Before dinner time,
it's good to reflect and relax.
A nice hot bath is just what you need,
to take your self-care to the max!

Just as water is life,
milk is that to a young one,
So let's draw up a milk-infused bath,
to celebrate rebirth and rejuvenation.

If you don't have a bathtub, no problem,
use a goatmilk's soap in the shower.
You can also make a milky face mask instead,
or drink tea made of the milk thistle flower!

Whatever you do,
take some time out to chill!
It'll leave you feeling rejuvenated,
I promise it will!

For Imbolc dinner -
you'll need a plate and a bowl!
There's so many soups to choose from,
you're going to want to try them all!

We have corn chowder, chicken noodle soup,
seafood bisque, minestrone, and beef stew!
We are serving pretzel knots, chicken wings,
a root vegetable shepherds pie,
baked and mashed potatoes,
with beet or bean salad on the side!

See, back before electricity or refrigerators,
it was hard to get fresh foods for the feast.
Therefore they turned to serving leftovers,
soups, root vegetables, and cured meats.

Imbolc proves you don't need fancy food -
This rustic spread is just as good!

As for Imbolc dessert,
there are many treats made with cream.
Whether in a puff pastry or a pie,
milk remains the theme!

A cream cheese no-bake tart,
cream puffs and éclairs,
crème brûlée broiled just right,
and so many cannolis to share!

A chocolate tres leches cake,
sweet, caramelly flan,
peanut butter cookies for a variety,
hot chocolate, and cream horns!

And if you can't have milk,
don't you worry!
To be inclusive for our guests,
we made quite a few things non-dairy!

After eating, it's game time,
and we're playing an Imbolc specialty.
The game is called Burrow Roll;
It's a sport of chance and possibility!

You'll need a specialty die,
the kind that goes up to three - not six,
and ask that each person who plans to play,
bring with them three very tiny gifts.
Those gifts go into uniform boxes,
and get mixed up on the table a bit.

The number each player rolls with the die,
is the number of gifts they can take.
And did I mention, as the host,
you'll also box up a toy swan and snake...

If someone gets the toy snake,
they can take a gift from another.
Whoever gets the toy swan,
keeps all the unclaimed prizes leftover!

As the night settles down,
I like to sit and admire this space,
humbled by the foliage of winter,
that enhance the beauty of my fireplace!

A pipberry branch garland,
speckled in shades of pink and blue,
with properties of intuition, water,
endless possibilities, and honoring the moon.

Pinecones tied with ribbons,
of brown and silver hues,
known to have properties of rejuvenation,
good luck, and unlocking potential, too.

There is less variety of foliage,
especially this time of year,
but when the few plants are brought together,
it's a sight I absolutely cherish.

And as I bid you farewell,
I leave you with one final tradition,
it's the act of gift giving -
But with specific conditions.

The presents you give must be clothing,
whether it be a shirt, pants, scarf, or shoes...
Place overnight near a water feature,
indoor or outdoor, either way is cool.

To make sure the gift is relevant,
consider if they have upcoming events,
like a dress for a dance, or a robe for the spa,
they'll know your gift is well-meant!

It's a nice way to wrap up Imbolc,
with something to wear on another day;
A festive method to commemorate,
celebrating this wintery holiday!

Happy Imbolc,
to you and yours!

Blessed Be
and Good Night.